Classic
AMERICAN CARS

The history, origins, and greats

CLASSIC AMERICAN CARS

Published by World Publications Group, Inc.
140 Laurel Street
East Bridgewater, MA 02333
www.wrldpub.com

© Instinctive Product Development 2013

Packaged by Instinctive Product Development for World Publications Group, Inc.

Printed in China

ISBN: 978-1-4643-0286-2

Designed by: BrainWave

Creative Director: Kevin Gardner

Written by: Charlie Morgan

Images courtesy of PA Photos, Magic Car Pics, Mary Evans Picture Library, and Wiki Commons

www.maryevans.com

Introduction

The obsession with creating a vehicle that was not reliant on the use of animals, capable of transporting people and goods, began in earnest in the second half of the 18th century. Those early pioneers utilized the latest development of steam-powered engines to provide the energy to move their inventions; some even began experimenting with electric vehicles – perhaps somewhat ironic considering the pressure manufacturers have been facing in recent years to develop affordable, sustainable, zero emissions vehicles to alleviate the world's dependence on fossil fuels. But the birth of the first practical internal combustion-engined automobile was credited to Karl Benz, who began production in 1888 in Mannheim, Germany. Fellow countrymen Gottlieb Daimler and Wilhelm Maybach soon swelled the ranks the following year, with the first vehicle that was purposely designed to be an automobile from the outset rather than a horse-drawn carriage that had been equipped with an engine.

This had all taken place in Europe, but the United States was not far behind and would soon grow to become the largest automobile-manufacturing nation in the world. This was partly driven by the size of the country and the population but also the innovators who lived there. In the late 19th century, a network of canals and railroads was already expanding, but the biggest change to the country – and indeed the world – would be the development of roads.

Drivers of the earliest automobiles were hindered and

■ ABOVE: Gottlieb Daimler, left, (1834-1900) and Karl Benz, right, (1844-1929) developed early automobiles in Germany.

■ OPPOSITE: A highway under construction in the United States.

■ BELOW: A road in Montauk, Long Island, New York, 1910.

restricted as to where they could go by the lack of usable roads, which were usually dirt tracks whose condition became impassable in bad weather. This all changed with the Federal Aid Road Act (1916) that provided $75 million, and further funding was allocated by the Federal Aid Highway Act of 1921, so that by 1924 the United States could boast 31,000 miles of surfaced road. This network was further expanded during the Eisenhower administration of the 1950s that ordered the construction of interstate highways and, of course, as the road network improved so automobiles became faster.

As the 19th century morphed into the 20th, more and more manufacturers were entering the market. The first National Automobile Show was held in

The automobile industry presents its National Automobile Show in New York City in 1912.

New York City's Madison Square in 1900, with 51 exhibitors showing off their wares to almost 50,000 visitors. But many of these manufacturers dropped by the wayside or were merged into other companies so that by the end of the 1920s the industry was dominated by the Big Three of Chrysler, Ford, and General Motors.

Henry Ford had been building automobiles since 1896, but the Ford Motor Company was not

■ ABOVE: The automobile industry presents its National Automobile Show in New York City in 1912.

set up until 1903 – a revolution was soon under way. The Model T arrived in 1908, but it was the introduction of conveyor-belt assembly lines five years later that truly changed the automobile industry and transformed Ford into the largest manufacturer in the US. By the time production of the Model T ceased in 1927, more than 15 million had been sold and manufacturing had already been outsourced to

(Australia, 1931) to become the world's largest automobile company.

The youngest of the Big Three was Chrysler that was set up by former Buick president and GM executive Walter Chrysler. He acquired the Maxwell Motor Company in 1920 and transformed it into Chrysler Corporation five years later before adding Dodge to his stable. By the time the 1930s had arrived, the Plymouth and DeSoto marques had been launched and Chrysler had overtaken Ford to become the second largest manufacturer.

As the industry grew, so did the workforce, with tens of thousands of jobs being created, but the Great Depression of the 1930s hit automobile manufacturing just as much as the rest of the country, and many smaller companies went out of business. Demand grew following the Second World War, with the automobile becoming an essential household (and business) item. This led to Americans becoming more mobile and meant that families could live further away from their workplace, resulting in a housing boom as the construction of suburbs outside city limits dramatically increased.

Australia, England, and Germany. General Motors Corporation was founded in 1908 and quickly absorbed established manufacturers such as Buick, Cadillac, Oakland (which would become Pontiac), and Oldsmobile. A merger with Ford fell through but GM carried on with their expansion program with the acquisition of Chevrolet, and foreign manufacturers Vauxhall Motors (England in 1925), Opel (Germany, 1929), and Holden

■ ABOVE: Henry Ford pictured in 1904.

■ BELOW: The 25,000 employees of the Ford Motor Company, Detroit, Michigan, USA, pose for a group photograph in front of the factory buildings. At the time, this was the largest group of employees ever gathered before a photographer at the (then) largest automobile works in the world – producing 1,000 automobiles a day.

■ ABOVE: In 1913, Henry Ford installed the first moving assembly line in his Highland Park factory (Detroit, Michigan) and startled the automobile industry by producing a car every 93 minutes. At the end of five years, the Highland Park plant was turning out 10,000 cars a day.

■ BELOW: Walter Chrysler (1875-1940), automobile magnate.

Japanese automobiles arrived in the United States at the end of the 1950s, and within 20 years the US manufacturers were forced to rethink their models to compete with the more fuel-efficient imports… especially following the Arab-Israeli war in 1973 and the ensuing oil embargo that saw gasoline prices rising disproportionately. By the end of the 1970s, Chrysler was in serious financial trouble and had to get a $1.5 billion loan guarantee from the US government.

The automobile industry in the

United States was overtaken as the world leader by Japan in the 1980s, with more than 25 per cent of the 40 million vehicles produced worldwide. By 2011, this total production figure had grown to more than 80 million worldwide, with the US lagging in third behind China and Japan. By this time, the Big Three were all suffering financially and both GM and Chrysler had received bailouts from the US government. Restructuring and cost cutting was the order of the day, but would it be enough to survive? Only time will tell…

The Coupe $715 f. o. b. Flint, Mich.

An Economical Quality Car of Great Utility

An unusually smart coupe with Body by Fisher, finished in lustrous Duco, with construction and appointments characteristic of cars of finest quality. Perfectly adapted to business or personal service—a good companion for your larger car.

CHEVROLET MOTOR COMPANY, DETROIT, MICHIGAN
Division of General Motors Corporation

Prices f. o. b. Flint, Michigan   Touring $525   Roadster $525 · Coach $735
Sedan $825   Commercial Chassis $425   Express Truck Chassis $550

QUALITY AT LOW COST

■ ABOVE: An advertisement for the Chevrolet coupe in the early 20th century.

AMC Gremlin

Designed by Richard A. Teague and Bob Nixon, this small two-door hatchback hit the road on April 1, 1970. Produced in Wisconsin, US, Ontario, Canada, and Mexico City, it was classed as a subcompact car and designed as part of American Motors Corporation's (AMC) remit for new small cars, with a shortened Hornet platform and a Kammback-type tail. Unveiled at a time when imports into the US provided stiff competition, the Gremlin was considered a sound economical purchase, although some derided its design.

The car was marketed as "America's first subcompact," although that honor should really go to the Crosley, but it was popular with buyers who were attracted by the price and it proved a comfortable driving machine. Two options were available in 1970 – a two-seater with fixed back window costing $1,879 and a four-seater with opening rear window that sported a price tag of $1,959. It was faster than other subcompact cars of the time and, although it was rather front heavy, it was considered easy to handle. It had a front-engine, rear-wheel-drive layout (FR), and debuted with a straight-six-cylinder 99 ci (3.3 L) engine, a seven main bearing design that produced 128 hp

■ **BELOW: The 1971 AMC Gremlin, shown in 1970.**

article cited that it provided an outstanding performance for an economy car. Over the life of the Gremlin, between 1970 and 1978, modifications were made and performance increased. Offered as an option in 1970, the 232 ci engine became standard in 1971. A V8 engine was introduced in 1972 and the base two-seater model was discontinued. The bumpers were strengthened for the 1973 model and sales grew by 30 per cent on 1972 figures. The side body stripes, offered as part of the "X" package introduced in 1971, took on a hockey stick shape in 1974 and, by 1975, standard electronic ignition was included. Greater changes came in 1976, with a four-speed manual transmission, and further modifications were made in 1977, including shortening the front end by four inches. In 1978, sales of the Gremlin fell by 52 per cent but an impressive 671,475 had been built by the time the car ceased production.

■ **BELOW: AMC releasing the 1974 model of the Gremlin.**

as standard. The option came as a 232 ci (3.8 L) straight-six engine that produced 145 hp.

It was rated by Tom McCahill in *Mechanic Illustrated* in 1970 as: "…the best American buy of the year," when the option engine made zero to 60 mph in 11.9 seconds and managed 100 mph on the Daytona Speedway. *Car and Driver* magazine confirmed McCahill's findings, while another

AMC Rambler

The AMC Rambler (also known as the Rambler American) evolved from the Rambler that Nash Motors had been manufacturing between 1950 and 1957 when they merged with the Hudson Motor Car Company to create American Motors Corporation in 1954. The 1958 recession convinced AMC that it needed to add a small compact to its range, particularly if they wanted to challenge the Big Three, but financial constraints meant that they were not in a position to develop a completely new model from scratch. They therefore revived the basis of their defunct Rambler and modified the design to produce the Rambler American, frequently the most affordable US-built car during its lifetime and popular for its economy.

The model made its debut in January 1958 – initially only as a two-door sedan – with slight modifications to its predecessor, and boasted a 195.6 ci (3.2 L) straight-

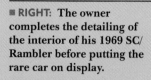

■ RIGHT: The owner completes the detailing of the interior of his 1969 SC/Rambler before putting the rare car on display.

■ BELOW: The AMC Rambler is shown in Chicago, 1958.

in 1961. The following year saw an alternative to the fully automatic transmission offered with the "E-stick" that paired an automatic clutch with a three-speed manual. Trim levels had been enhanced over the years and, by 1963, the top of the range was the 440-H, complete with adjustable front bucket seats.

The Rambler American was totally revamped for the third and final generation as it took on a modern appearance more suited to the 1960s, and there was a lot more choice for the consumer with a range of body styles, transmissions, and engines. As the decade progressed, rounded corners were squared off and safety measures introduced in accordance with US National Highway Traffic Safety Administration (NHTSA) regulations before the range was replaced by the AMC Hornet, with more than 4.2 million vehicles having been sold.

One variant that has proved extremely collectible was the Hurst SC/Rambler, a muscle car powered by a 390 cu (6.4 L) V8 engine that was advertised to run the quarter mile in 14.3 seconds.

six engine producing 90 hp. A new grille and reworked fender wells were the most obvious changes, and discerning buyers were given two choices: the base Deluxe for $1,789 or the Super, priced at $1,879. The following year a two-door station wagon was introduced – that accounted for more than 35 per

cent of the total Rambler American sales in 1959 – before the arrival of a four-door sedan in 1960.

The second generation Rambler American was slightly narrower and shorter than its predecessor and took on a more angular body style, while a four-door station wagon and two-door convertible were added

Cadillac De Ville

The Cadillac De Ville was one of the most enduring models in the company's history, with production running through eight generations from 1959 until 2005. The name originally designated a level of trim and was first applied to the luxury Series 62 Coupe De Ville in 1949, one of the first pillarless hardtop coupes ever produced. A sedan version was introduced in 1956 and, when sales of the Sedan De Ville exceeded its Series 62 counterpart, it was only a matter of time before the De Ville became a model name in its own right with the launch of the first generation, originally labeled the Series 6300.

The inaugural De Ville typified automobile styling of the 1950s, with impressive tailfins and twin bullet-shaped taillights, and was powered by a 390 ci (6.4 L) OHV V8 engine. The list of standard equipment was impressive and included power steering, power brakes, power windows, power seats, and two-speed windshield wipers. From 1960, the body styling received a smoother treatment, with the tailfins being somewhat downsized while the amount of chrome was toned down.

The second generation, introduced in 1961, received a gentle facelift and saw the addition of a shorter Town six-window hardtop – only available during 1961 before being replaced by the Park Avenue four-window hardtop. The next couple of years saw the hardtop range being standardized to four-window vehicles, the engine was modified without changing the output or displacement, while 1964 saw the first convertible. The same year, a 429 ci (7 L) engine was also made available.

Further changes in body style occurred as the De Ville aged gracefully, with the tailfins being made smaller until they finally disappeared altogether. The fifth generation, launched in 1977,

■ **ABOVE:** A 1959 Cadillac red rear tail rocket.
■ **BELOW:** A Cadillac Coupe De Ville, 1949.

was notable for being the first De Villes to be sold without fender skirts half covering the rear wheels. By this time, the range had been slimmed down and the only options available were a two-door coupe or a four-door sedan. A wider choice of engines was also on offer in the 350 ci (5.7 L) Diesel V8, a 252 ci (4.1 L) V6, or a 250 ci (4.1 L) V8. The 1980s saw the De Ville adopt a front-wheel-drive system and the start of shared body platforms in the C-body (with the Fleetwood variant) and the K-body (with the Seville in 1994). From the latter half of the 1990s, the only body style available was a four-door sedan, and the final De Ville emerged in June 2005 before being replaced by the Cadillac DTS (De Ville Touring Sedan).

15

Cadillac Eldorado

The Cadillac Eldorado made its debut in 1953 and spent the next half-century as one of the company's flagship luxury models. Like the De Ville, the Eldorado started life as part of the Series 62 range but was launched in its own right (in 1959). It was initially only available as a two-door convertible special edition that included wire wheels and a wraparound windshield, but 1954 saw the second generation share more components with other Cadillacs and a two-door hardtop coupe was introduced two years

later in the Eldorado Seville with the convertible now marketed as the Eldorado Biarritz. The original 331 ci (5.4 L) OHV V8 was joined by a 365 ci (6.0 L) OHV V8 engine, and the ubiquitous tailfins put in their first appearance.

The body styling received a revised rear end in 1957, the same year that the Series 70 Eldorado Brougham made its debut. The Brougham was a limited, hand-built edition that introduced quad headlights for the first time and boasted a unique trim level. The four-door hardtop was marketed

as the ultimate in luxury and was priced at $13,074… more than a Rolls-Royce Silver Cloud. Needless to say, only 400 were sold that year, with 304 leaving the dealers' showrooms in 1958. The Eldorado gained its independence from the Series 62 in 1959, while the Seville bade its farewell the following year and the Brougham was given its own unique series.

The 1960s saw the Eldorado convertible sold as part of the De Ville series until 1964, when it was then brought under the Fleetwood mantle. Like other manufacturers,

Cadillac styling was evolving and the Eldorado was no exception with smoother, square lines replacing the exaggerated angles of its ancestors. Sharing a platform with the Oldsmobile Tornado, the Eldorado took its bow as the first front-wheel-drive Cadillac in 1967, but the seventh generation was only available as a two-door hardtop.

As the 1970s wore on, automobile manufacturers began sharing more and more components between vehicles to cut costs, and the Eldorado was no exception, being related to the Tornado and the Buick Riviera. The following decade saw the Eldorado downsized, with the convertible being finally discontinued in 1986, although it was lengthened for the final generation in 1992. Sales were falling, however, and production of the Eldorado ceased in 2002.

■ **LEFT: A Cadillac Eldorado, standing outside of New York's Tavern on the Green restaurant in Central Park, 1958.**

■ **BELOW: A white Cadillac Eldorado Biarritz convertible, 1958.**

Checker

One of the most iconic and instantly recognizable cars of all time, yet probably not on many classic car buyers' wish list, the Checker deserves to be included in this collection of American classic cars. The Checker Cab Manufacturing Company was set up in May 1922, at a time when rival cab firms could be ruthless when it

■ **ABOVE:** A vintage New York City Checker cab waits for a fare.

■ **OPPOSITE:** Kalamazoo's Checker Cab production ended in 1982. The Gilmore Car Museum began in 1963 and is a public, non-profit educational institution dedicated to preserving the history and heritage of the American automobile.

came to winning fares. It all started when Morris Markin – the son of a poor Russian tailor – found himself taking over possession of an auto-body manufacturing firm (following a friend's default on a $15,000 personal loan), which he named Markin Automobile Body. They supplied Commonwealth Motors, who in turn were contracted to

Great Depression hit Checker as it did all other walks of life, with sales being restricted to cash on delivery. November 1931 saw the situation improve with a 1,000-unit order from Chicago Yellow Cabs, and the Series T and Series Y were brought in before the Second World War – although it would be the Series A (1940) that boasted the greatest longevity in its various guises.

The A8 arrived in 1956 and boasted a brand new body that would remain the company standard. Checker dabbled in "civilian" autos but, when the Superba Special was renamed the Marathon in 1961, the recipe for success had been perfected. The Marathon became synonymous with yellow cabs and proved a bestseller for Checker throughout the 1960s and 1970s. The relaxing of cab regulations by New York City, however, in the early 1970s, allowing operators to use conventional sedans, was a deathblow for Checker. The Big Three could offer cabs at a much cheaper price and, although the company initially struggled on, production finally ceased in 1982.

Checker Taxi of Chicago (later the Yellow Cab Company), and a legend was born, with Markin soon owning all three firms.

Initial production targets called for three vehicles to be completed a day but, by January 1923, the assembly line was running 24 hours a day and 112 cabs were rolling out a month. Within three months, the plant had relocated to Kalamazoo, Michigan, and a 700-strong workforce was ensuring that the Checker cab became a familiar sight. The following year saw sales hitting 4,000 as the Series E was introduced as a Landau or limousine model. Further new models arrived with the Series K (1929) and Series M (1930), but the

Chevrolet Bel Air

■ ABOVE: A Chevrolet Bel Air Sport coupe, 1956.

The Bel Air moniker first appeared on Chevrolet's Styleline Deluxe, the company's first hardtop, and it wasn't until 1953 that it became a series in its own right. It is perhaps difficult to comprehend now, but hardtops hadn't sold particularly well until they were designed as a convertible with a fixed solid roof offering the best of both worlds, according to Chevrolet's advertising: "open to the summer breeze… snug against the wintry wind." Like Chevrolet, Buick, Cadillac, and Oldsmobile had introduced hardtops in 1949, but neither Chrysler nor Ford had dipped their toe in that particular market yet. While the first generation Bel Air was considered by many to be "durable yet dull," the revised models (150, 210, and Delray) that appeared in 1955, couldn't have been further removed.

Arriving as rock'n'roll was taking the United States by storm, the Bel Air – nicknamed the "Hot One" in the company's advertising – was aesthetically pleasing in hardtop, convertible, or station wagon (Nomad) versions. The introduction of Chevrolet's first V8 engine in 35 years saw the 265 ci (4.3 L) Turbo-Fire go on to earn legendary status as the company finally found the right vehicle to counter Ford's dominance.

Whereas the initial Bel Airs had been at the top of the Chevrolet range, from the mid-1950s onward they were positioned right in the middle. No longer were they seen as automobiles for middle-aged drivers; the Bel Air was the coolest thing on the strip. The sleek lines and Ferrari-inspired grille, combined with restrained tailfins and a modicum of chrome, ensured that the 1955-57 Bel Airs would go on to become some of the most collectible in American history.

The Bel Air was revised for 1958 – a 348 ci (5.7 L) engine was now an option – but received a major makeover the following year that gave it a truly unique styling. The chunky body of its predecessor had given way to an elongated vision of the future, with wing-shaped tailfins. The headlights had been positioned as low as legislation would allow and the rear end now sported a pair of cats-eye taillights. As the 1960s dawned, the sweeping lines of the Bel Air were toned down to be more in touch with society's expectations of an automobile and this trend continued until the line was discontinued in 1975.

Chevrolet's striking Bel Air Sport Coupe. With 3 great new series, Chevrolet offers the widest choice of models in its field.

How Chevrolet's new high-compression horsepower takes you more places on less gas . . .

You see *two* pretty exciting kinds of horsepower in our picture up there.

One is the rarin', buckin', four-legged kind that makes a rodeo a popular place to go.

The other kind is the smooth, quiet horsepower of that spankin' new Chevrolet.

The beauty of Chevrolet's new power is this: It gives you greater acceleration, and passing ability. More "steam" for steep hills. And all on less gas—a lot less gas. And on *regular* gas at that!

How can you get more power on less gas? High compression is the answer. The fuel mixture is squeezed much tighter so that the engine wrings much more power out of it.

Chevrolet brings you the benefits of high-compression power whether you choose the mighty 115-h.p. "Blue-Flame" engine teamed with Powerglide* automatic transmission or the advanced 108-h.p. "Thrift-King" engine with standard transmission.

And Chevrolet brings you much more you'll like besides. Why not stop in soon and let your nearby Chevrolet dealer show you. . . . Chevrolet Division of General Motors, Detroit 2, Michigan.

Optional at extra cost. Combination of Powerglide automatic transmission and 115-h.p. "Blue-Flame" engine available on "Two-Ten" and Bel Air models only.

MORE PEOPLE BUY CHEVROLETS THAN ANY OTHER CAR!

■ ABOVE: The Chevrolet Bel Air coupe is the car to drive if you're attending a rodeo in the West.

Chevrolet Camaro

The music world might have been reverberating to the Beach Boys' *Pet Sounds* album, but the streets of the United States were throbbing to another unforgettable noise and 1966 will forever be remembered as the year that Chevrolet launched their Camaro into the pony car market with its main rival being the Ford Mustang. The Mustang had enjoyed runaway success after its arrival in 1964, with Ford enjoying their best sales for a new model for more than 30 years. Launched with a starting price of $2,466, the base Camaro was slightly cheaper than the average $2,650 new car.

The long-hooded 2+2 shared its F-body platform with its sister vehicle, the Pontiac Firebird, and its FR configuration pitted it squarely against the Mustang. Offered in just two body styles – coupe or convertible – the Camaro was designed to accommodate a variety of engines that could be married to an equally wide range of transmissions, from a three- or four-speed manual to a two-speed Powerglide automatic that was replaced by a three-speed Hydramatic option.

■ **OPPOSITE: An advertisement for the Chevrolet Camaro.**
■ **BELOW: A 1968 Chevrolet Camaro warms up ahead of a burnout contest during a car rally, 2006.**

The second generation Camaro arrived in February 1970, and was the recipient of heavy restyling (which was further tinkered with in 1974 and 1978) that increased the vehicle's size – both in terms of length and width – as well as the weight. The body was sleeker and the suspension had been improved, but the convertible option had disappeared and would not return until 1987. Still, the Camaro sold well and was developed throughout the 1970s before the range was totally revamped for 1982.

Fuel injection was available, as was a four-cylinder engine, following the previous decade's oil crises, and the coupe had been

transformed into a hatchback with MacPherson struts replacing the previous front subframe and a torque arm with coil springs taking the place of the rear leaf springs. A popular model was the Camaro Z28 – *Motor Trend* magazine's Car of the Year for 1982 – used as the pace car for that year's Indianapolis 500

– and demand was high, with more than 6,000 replicas being sold.

Sales of the fourth generation (introduced in 1993) were slowing as the 20th century came to a close and production ceased in 2002, the year that Chevrolet marked 35 years of the Camaro with a special edition that was only available as a Targa top

(T-top) or convertible. Enthusiasts were overjoyed, however, when Chevrolet relaunched the Camaro in 2009. Unashamedly basing its looks on the 1969 model, the latest Camaro received rave reviews and – true to its heritage – the base car's $23,000 price tag was still cheaper than the $29,217 average.

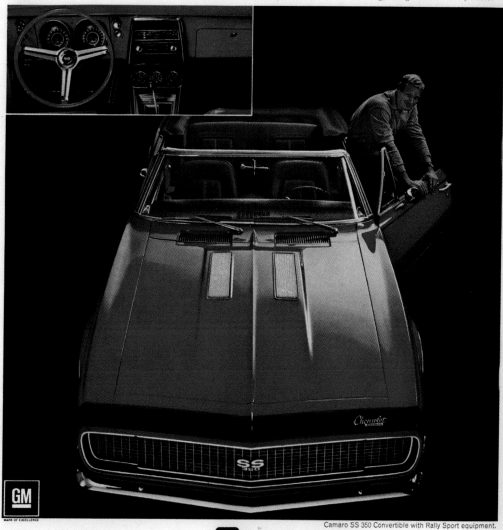

Chevrolet Corvette

Despite the fact that General Motors dominated the US market in the early 1950s, accounting for more than half of the vehicles sold, the company didn't have a sports car in their portfolio. When GM head of styling Harley Earl and his team of designers came up with the Chevrolet Corvette in 1953, however, they could hardly have dreamt that their creation would still be going strong 60 years later.

Over the intervening years, the Corvette has gone through six generations – the eagerly awaited next incarnation postponed after GM's financial difficulties at the end of the 2000s – and sold almost two million units on its way to becoming the most popular sports car in the United States.

Named after a series of Second World War small, fast naval ships, the Corvette debuted in New York City in January 1953, and its body construction proudly showed off the latest fiberglass technology. While they might have looked the part, the first Corvettes lacked the power to thrill, with a 235 ci (4.3 L) 150 hp engine and a two-speed automatic transmission based on what was essentially a 1952 Chevrolet sedan chassis, although 300 were sold in the first year of production. That seems somewhat surprising given its $3,498 price tag compared to the average car's $1,650 cost, but what the first generation lacked in performance its successor more than made up for.

The second generation (1963-67), which introduced the Stingray, are still regarded by many enthusiasts as the best Corvettes ever produced. A fastback coupe version was added with a rear window that could best be described as being shaped like a boat tail. In answer to the performance issues, the suspension was revamped and a 396 ci (6.5 L) 435 hp engine was offered from 1965. The longest running of the Corvette series was the third generation that was available between 1968 and 1982, with more than 540,000 vehicles being sold during the 14-year period although – like many manufacturers during the 1970s – emission regulations and oil prices led to performance being downgraded.

The 1984-96 Corvettes suffered

■ ABOVE: The Corvette Stingray Sport coupe, 1963.
■ OPPOSITE: The Corvette C1, 1959.
■ BELOW: The Corvette ZR1, 2009.

initial quality issues that hindered sales, but GM have reinstated the Corvette as America's most coveted sports car since then with smooth, elegant body styling that hints at the power lying beneath its sultry exterior. Indeed, the Corvette ZR1 – launched in December 2007 – boasted a new LS9 378 ci (6.2 L) engine that produced 638 hp to break the 200 mph (320 kmh) barrier.

25

Chevrolet Impala

The Impala name has been a staple ingredient of the Chevrolet range since 1958 – not in continuous production – although its position within the company has waxed and waned much like its reputation. The Impala began life as the Chevrolet flagship model when it was introduced as the top-of-the-range Bel Air in 1958. Two body styles were initially available in the convertible and hardtop coupe – both typical of the 1950s with sweeping rooflines, tailfins, and sculptured rear fenders – and the following year Chevrolet launched the Impala as a standalone series.

■ ABOVE: A Chevrolet Impala Sport coupe, 1958.

The second generation received the same treatment as the Bel Air, with the body being given a low and wide styling finished off by tailfins that resembled a bat's wing, as hardtops and sedans joined the Impala family, while a station wagon completed the range in 1961. By this time, the Impala had been restyled on the B-platform – shared with the Bel Air and Biscayne – and the Super Sport had been launched that boasted a 409 ci (6.7 L) 340 hp engine.

The Impala was gaining in popularity and hit an all-time high in 1965, when more than one

If elegance is understatement, you're looking at the understatement of the year.

Impala Custom Coupe.
Even sounds exclusive, doesn't it? Like something outrageously expensive, made for the "I-always-go-first-class" individuals.
To the first-class part: yes. But outrageously expensive? Hardly. Chevrolet builds it.
Now look again. At what makes the Custom Coupe elegant. At the distinctive roof line, so like a limousine. At its full door-glass styling. At its massive grille.

But Impala's good taste also comes from what we left off: the rampant slashes of chrome some cars tack on to justify their price. (We've got a name for cars that claim they're in the same class. Social climbers.)
Impala Custom Coupe is just what it sounds like. And, certainly, the people who buy it have money to spend. On other things. **CHEVROLET**
Putting you first, keeps us first.

million were sold… a record that still stands today. The extensively redesigned fourth generation came with a bewildering choice of engines that included a 250 ci (4.1 L) straight-six and nine V8s ranging from 283 ci (4.6 L) to the massive 454 ci (7.4 L), but the introduction of the Caprice would eventually have a detrimental impact on the Impala, which soon found itself slipping down the Chevrolet range.

After a successful revamp in 1971, the Impala convertible was dropped the following year, which also brought unleaded gas

with its accompanying reduction in power and performance. The remainder of the oil-scarce 1970s saw the Impala considerably downsized, and smaller V6 engines (as well as a diesel) were offered as manufacturers strived to make their autos more efficient and economical. By the time the Impala name was dropped in 1985 (although its sister Caprice continued until 1990), the range had slipped down the Chevrolet listing until it was basically a full-sized entry-level model.

The Impala was back, briefly, between 1994 and 1996, when

the SS tag was applied to a high performance Caprice in an effort to boost sales, but it wasn't until 2000 that the Impala SS became a permanent residence in the Chevrolet garage. Since then, it has undergone several transformations and the 10th generation was unveiled at the New York Auto Show in March 2013, described by GM as "a reestablishment of a popular, enduring, and iconic nameplate with a new outlook on style, comfort, efficiency, and safety."

■ **ABOVE: An advertisement for the Chevrolet Impala.**

Chrysler 300 Series

Launched in 1955 as a low production run, high performance, luxury auto, Chrysler designated their 300 series (not to be confused with their later 300 non-letter series that ran from 1962 until 1971) by letter to denote the year of manufacture. The name may have been resurrected for the 21st century 300M and the 300C but these modern vehicles bear no relation to the classics that were developed after the Second World War.

The range was actually launched as the C-300 (describing the 300 hp) with a 331 ci (5.4 L) V8 engine and was essentially a racecar designed for the National Association for Stock Car Auto Racing (NASCAR) circuits. In order to qualify, Chrysler had to produce a limited number of vehicles for public use to satisfy homologation purposes and 1,725 were built in the first year. The design team were restricted by a lack of funding so used the front end of an Imperial, the hardtop two-door body shell from a New Yorker, with the rear quarter from a Windsor, to create an icon. Options were limited, with three choices of exterior color, but tan leather was standard interior décor. With the subsequent "lettering" of each year's model, the C-300 is now considered by many to be the 300A.

Little changed for 1956's 300B, but the following year saw the 300C receive new styling and a convertible was introduced to see out the 1950s. The 300F of 1960 saw a radical redesign of the body, using Chrysler's new lightweight unibody, while the engine was now enlarged to 413 ci (6.8 L) and boasted a power output of 375 hp. The tailfins, which had been becoming more exaggerated, disappeared altogether in 1962 when Chrysler introduced its 300 Sport Series to run alongside, but production numbers had dropped considerably with only 570 vehicles leaving the factory. That plummeted to just 400 the following year when there was no convertible option for the 300J (Chrysler had decided to omit the "I" in case people confused it with a "1").

The 300K was marketed as both coupe and convertible but the biggest difference was in cost, with less impressive specifications to the interior upholstery and engine bringing the cost down by more than $1,000. A record 3,647 were produced in 1964, but the range was discontinued the following year as all the refinements that made the 300L so special were offered as extras on the normal 300.

■ ABOVE: The Chrysler 300, 1969.

■ RIGHT: The interior of a Chrysler 300 with its basic options.

There have been numerous models of Dodge that carried the Charger name but for the majority of enthusiasts the classic is the rear-wheel-drive coupe and muscle car that was produced on the B-body platform between 1966 and 1978 (although the latter models were based on the Chrysler Cordoba). The company's intention was to create a sporty-looking fastback to sit between the Ford Mustang and the higher end Thunderbird while utilizing as many existing components as possible to keep costs to a minimum – the Coronet was chosen as the donor vehicle.

Fastbacks had been extremely popular between the wars but had fallen out of favor with the advent of the "hardtop convertible." The trend for massive tailfins, however, wouldn't last long and the sleek aerodynamics of the fastback were soon a major selling point. It also meant that a manufacturer could make several different models out of essentially the same parts with just the roof, tail, and decklid differing.

Apart from being based on the Coronet, every aspect of the Dodge Charger had been impeccably thought through. The headlights revolved through 180 degrees to become almost invisible when switched off, while the interior boasted four bucket seats (with the rear pair folding down to create a large carpeted cargo area). The full-length console that divided the car in half was equally as impressive and contained a lit storage bin under the front armrest. All in all, the design team had come up with a spectacular vehicle powered by a choice of V8 engines that sold more

This beautiful new bomb comes from the drawing board to your driveway with all the excitement left in. It's Dodge Charger, and it's loaded. With fresh ideas, eye-tempting styling, explosive performance. "What a handsome home for a Hemi!" you say? We thought you would—so a big, bad 426 Street Hemi is optional. In a package deal with a heavy-duty suspension—0.92-inch torsion bars, link-type sway bar, high-rate rear springs and heavy-duty shocks—to keep you firmly in control. Plus 11-inch brakes and 4-ply nylon Blue Streak tires for extra safety. Add to the package with options like a heavy-duty TorqueFlite automatic transmission (set for full-throttle shifts at 5500 rpm) or a competition-type, 4-speed manual gearbox. Check out Charger, the hot new one from Dodge that proves sports cars can also be luxurious.

■ ABOVE: A Dodge Charger, 1966.

Dodge Charger

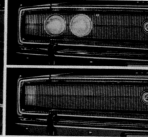

...ever had it so luxurious, sports. Bucket seats, center ...le with padded armrest and full carpeting are just a ...andard '66 Dodge Charger comfort features.

Dodge Charger's tach is no add-on afterthought. It's right up next to the speedometer, where it belongs. The swivel clock mounted on the console is optional.

Charger's "now-you-see-'em, now-you-don't" headlights look great no matter what position they are in, and move into place automatically.

...a sporty-type car and a station wagon, and what happens? Charger! These handsome rear seats fold down to give you extra luggage space—enough to handle a pair of skiis.

A winner, going away. That's Dodge Charger, the new smoothy. And just as it packs a big punch under the hood up front, you'll find you can pack a big load under that clean, crisply styled rear deck lid. Fold the rear seats down, and you've got about 7½ feet of completely carpeted cargo space.
• YOU HAVE A CHANCE OF WINNING A DODGE CHARGER—REGISTER AT YOUR DODGE DEALER'S.

Dodge Charger
DODGE DIVISION ◆ CHRYSLER MOTORS CORPORATION

than 37,000 before the 1967 model was launched.

The second generation arrived in 1968 with a redesigned body – that has since become synonymous with the General Lee from *The Dukes of Hazzard* TV show (1979-85) – and an R/T (Road/Track) high performance package. Even though the interior had lost much of its previous charm and attraction with being made more basic (vinyl instead of carpet in the cargo area for instance), the Charger was still in favor and sold almost 100,000 units. The limited edition Charger 500 and Daytona appeared before the third generation made its debut in 1971.

While still bearing a resemblance to its predecessors, Dodge had now merged the Coronet and Charger, but the biggest redesign came in 1975 with the final Charger series. Now based on the Cordoba, the Charger lost its distinctive looks and became more traditional before it was replaced by the Magnum in 1978.

31

■ BELOW: **The General Lee from** *The Dukes of Hazzard* **sails over a stream. (Copyright: © Warner Bros. Pictures/Ronald Grant Archive/Mary Evans)**

Dodge Coronet

CORONET and CUSTOM

Either way,
you get a wagon full of extras.

Here are some wagons you'll welcome. The 1971 Coronet station wagons. There's one priced right for every family, depending on their degree of indulgence. This year, all Coronet wagons have the Dual Action tailgate, and all three-seat wagons have as standard equipment the Auto-Lock electric tailgate which prevents the door from accidentally opening when the ignition is on. Popular optional features include a "rear window cleaning vane" and "lockable rear luggage compartment." Of course, there's lots more. Check over the Standard and Optional Equipment Lists and you'll come up with the wagon that's styled, priced, and equipped just the way you want it. What wagon could be more welcome?

Coronet
wagon.

Coronet Custom
wagon.

STANDARD EQUIPMENT, WAGONS: 3-speed manual transmission, shift lever on steering column • Heater/defroster • 2-speed concealed wipers • Keyless Door Locking System • Foot-operated parking brake • 3-spoke color-keyed steering wheel • Glove box lock • Dome light • Torsion-bar front suspension • Cigarette lighter • Dual Action tailgate with concealed hinges • Manual lock on tailgate • Rear compartment cargo light (standard, 3-seat wagons; optional, 2-seat wagons) • Rear door automatic dome light switch (standard, Crestwood; optional, Coronet and Custom) • Simulated wood-grained instrument panel appliqué, with hooded, circular instrumentation including 150-mph speedometer, oil pressure and fuel gauges, temperature and alternator gauges (Crestwood) • Exterior simulated wood-grained overlay (Crestwood) • Color-keyed carpet for rear floor well (3-seat wagons) • Auto-Lock electric tailgate lock system (standard, 3-seat wagons) • Deluxe wheel covers (standard on Crestwood) • 225-cu.-in. Six (Coronet and Custom 3-seat wagons only) • 318 V8 (standard V8 on all Coronet wagons) • Color-keyed rubber floor mat (Coronet) • Color-keyed carpeting (Custom and Crestwood) • Vinyl front bench—Blue, Green, Tan, or Black interior trim colors (Coronet and Custom) • Vinyl split-back front bench with center armrest—Blue, Green, Tan, or Black interior trim colors (Crestwood only) • Color-keyed steering wheel with simulated wood-grained insert (standard, Custom and Crestwood; optional, Coronet).

The Dodge Coronet was one of the first new models to be introduced to the streets of America following the end of the Second World War. The full-size car was initially set as the highest trim but soon found itself relegated to the bottom of the division by the mid-1950s, and 1965 saw the Coronet reduced to a mid-size vehicle.

The first Coronet debuted with the bulbous curves and sweeping lines that were popular in the late 1940s and was powered by a 230 ci (3.8 L) flathead straight-six that provided refinement and power with a top speed of around 90 mph (140 kmh). The range offered

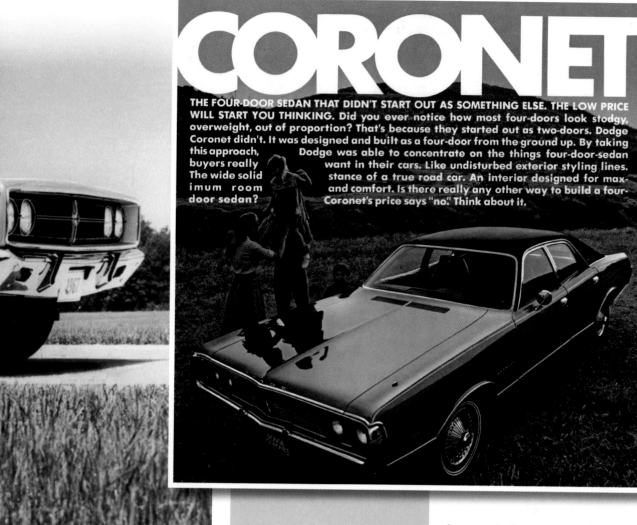

CORONET

THE FOUR-DOOR SEDAN THAT DIDN'T START OUT AS SOMETHING ELSE. THE LOW PRICE WILL START YOU THINKING. Did you ever notice how most four-doors look stodgy, overweight, out of proportion? That's because they started out as two-doors. Dodge Coronet didn't. It was designed and built as a four-door from the ground up. By taking this approach, Dodge was able to concentrate on the things four-door-sedan buyers really want in their cars. Like undisturbed exterior styling lines. The wide solid stance of a true road car. An interior designed for maximum room and comfort. Is there really any other way to build a four-door sedan? Coronet's price says "no." Think about it.

■ **ABOVE: A Coronet sedan, 1971.**

■ **LEFT: A Dodge Coronet, 1967.**

■ **OPPOSITE: A Coronet custom wagon, 1971.**

two-door coupes and hardtops with four-door sedans and station wagons, but also boasted the unique eight-seater limousine. Minor revisions took place before the arrival of the second generation in 1953 (and a 241 ci (3.9 L) V8 "Red Ram" engine) that would become famous with numerous landspeed records on the Bonneville Salt Flats. Despite including more luxury in their vehicles, Dodges did not sell in the quantities that parent company Chrysler were anticipating and they were forced to seek financial assistance.

The Dodge direction changed, with the 1955 Coronet being marketed at the lower trim level while the redesigned body – that was longer, wider, and lower – helped to boost sales. The introduction of the D-500 (1956) and D-501 (1957) Coronets, complete with typical 1950s tailfin styling, saw the company target the NASCAR scene before disappearing in 1959. The Coronet returned in 1965 as a mid-size vehicle that bore little resemblance to its ancestor.

Based on the Polara, the Coronet became the best-selling Dodge in 1965, with almost 210,000 sales, but it was as a muscle car that it would become a classic. The late 1960s saw the Coronet offered in R/T and Super Bee editions that were powered by the 426 ci (7.0 L) Hemi V8 that neared an output level of almost 400 hp. The body was completely redesigned in 1968 before the familial Coronet was merged with the Charger as Chrysler's model overlap became more and more integrated.

By 1971, the Coronet had become twinned with the Plymouth Satellite and had lost all its independence. It was only offered as a four-door sedan or station wagon and sales began to nosedive. The Coronet was finally retired in 1976 when the range was renamed Monaco.

33

Duesenberg Model J

The height of late-1920s opulence, the Duesenberg Model J was designed to be the "biggest, fastest and most expensive car ever made" and was intended to compete with rivals such as Rolls-Royce and Mercedes-Benz in the luxury grand touring car market. E. L. Cord was an entrepreneur in the fields of automobiles, aviation, and shipping who took control of the bankrupt Duesenberg Automobile & Motors Company Inc. in October 1926, and set Fred Duesenberg with the aforementioned challenge.

Sadly, the economic climate was not exactly ideal, with the Great Depression on the horizon that would stretch well into the 1930s, and by 1937 the Duesenberg marque was defunct. The initial target was to sell 500 units a year, but only 300 cars had been bought by the end of 1930.

Unlike mass production models, however, the Duesenberg was sold as just a chassis and running gear, with the body and interior being contracted out to one of numerous coachbuilders depending on the customer's preference. The power was originally provided by Duesenberg's straight-eight model J engine – with four valves per cylinder and dual overhead camshafts – that had proved its racing pedigree in the 1920s. The 420 ci (6.9 L) engine was advertised as being capable of a top speed of around 115 mph (185 kmh) with a 265 hp output, although fuel economy was obviously not high on the agenda with only 11 to 13 miles per gallon.

Cost was not an issue for those

even participated in advertising campaigns to try to boost sales for the ailing company. A total of 481 Model Js (including SJ, SSJ, JN, and SJN variants) were produced during the model's eight-year lifespan, and it is testament to its quality and reputation that an estimated 378 have survived into the 21st century. The Duesenberg Model J might be an octogenarian, but it still oozes star quality…

■ ABOVE: A Duesenberg Model J, 1929.

■ LEFT: A Duesenberg Model J, 1932.

■ BELOW: The dashboard of a 1929 Duesenberg Model J convertible coupe.

contemplating buying a Duesenberg though. The original chassis was priced at $8,500 in 1929 – at a time when the average car cost $425 – although the coachbuild would easily more than double the total for a finished car. One popular treatment was the Murphy Convertible Roadster which, in 1932, would have set the discerning owner back $11,000.

Advertised with the slogan "The World's Finest Motor Car," the Model J was a hit with the Hollywood elite, who

Ford Fairlane/Torino

To begin with, the Fairlane was Ford's full-size model when it was launched in 1955, but by 1962 it was the company's answer to the muscle car market. The Torino was a spin-off from the Fairlane, which came later on the drag strip.

The car was named after Fair Lane, Henry Ford's mansion in Dearborn, Michigan, and was offered in six body styles, including the plastic-topped Crown Victoria Skyliner. There was also a steel-top Victoria, hardtop coupe, and a convertible as

well as more traditional sedans.

The Fairlanes were distinguishable for their characteristic stainless-steel Fairlane stripe and optional two-tone paint. They were renowned for their solidity. It replaced the Crestline

■ RIGHT: A Ford
Fairlane, 1955.

■ BELOW: The Ford Fairlane
with hardtop folding roof
operation, 1957.

fairly static until the early 1960s, when Ford needed to compete in the muscle car market. These new emerging models were big business from the start, and Ford debuted its Fairlane Thunderbolt, designed for drag racing, in 1964. The Thunderbolt had a 427 ci (7.0 L) V8 race engine with Ram Air, fiberglass hood, doors, and fenders, and two four-barrel carburetors.

Further Fairlanes were added to the lines over the years up to 1970 when production ceased in North America. The Fairlane 500 was a base model that would ultimately lead to the Torino series. The Torino Cobra contained a large engine – a 429 ci (7.0 L) with four-barrel carburetor and 360 hp, although economy was offered with the straight-six engine. Racing slowed down a degree in the 1970s and Ford reverted to its older models.

When production ceased in the United States, the Falcon name was transferred to an intermediate platform version known as the "1970½," but the names Fairlane and Falcon were discontinued as the Torino came to prominence.

as a full-size model. In the car's second year in production, two more powerful V8 options were introduced, alongside a four-door Victoria hardtop and a Lifeguard package. The Fairlane was given a sleeker look in 1957, and the Fairlane 500 Skyliner, with a power retractable hardtop, made its debut. In 1958, quad headlights were added together with other changes in style. Apart from the introduction of the Ford Galaxie in 1959, the models remained

Ford Falcon

The Ford Falcon made its debut in 1960 and claimed the roads for a decade, with huge sales that rivaled the compact cars from General Motors and Chrysler. A wide range of body styles was offered including two-door, four-door sedans, station wagons, hardtops, and convertibles. There was, in addition, the Ranchero pickup. The name Falcon had come into existence in 1935 when Edsel Ford (Henry's son) designed a more luxurious car, which later became the Mercury, rather than the Falcon. The 1950s saw Ford competing with GM and Chrysler for the large, profitable car market across North America and Canada, but changed their individual strategies when it became clear that a new approach was needed toward the early 1960s. The mid-20th century saw more

■ ABOVE: A 1963 model Ford Falcon.
■ BELOW: A Ford Falcon GT.

Falcon GT

cars on the road – many American families were ready for a second, or third, vehicle – and the expensive gas-guzzlers found themselves competing with smaller, compact European models, particularly on pricing. It was this that led the Big Three to realize that they needed to maintain their competitive edge – and it would lead to the Ford Falcon.

While deemed a "small" car by American standards, the Falcon was established firmly in the mid-range by Robert S. McNamara. The soon-to-be vice president of Ford insisted that costs be kept as low as possible. A standard suspension was chosen and a unibody added to allow a comfortable ride for up to six passengers. The engine was a small, 90 hp, 144 ci (2.4 L) straight-six, while drum brakes were added all round the three-speed manual transmission, which came as standard. While the United States made its acquaintance with the Ford Falcon, the company's Canadian subsidiary launched the Frontenac in 1960. This was a Falcon-based model, designed to give Canadian dealers a smaller car for their markets. The Canadian version was only available for the 1960 model year, and was replaced the following year by the Mercury Comet. The second generation came in 1964 when the Falcon underwent a modern redesign that was aimed at the youth market. The Sprint package offered a 260 ci (4.3 L) V8 engine and loud exhaust (although pitched against the Mustang it never really took off). Convertible Falcons were dropped in 1965 due to falling sales, although other models gained power steering and seat belts as standard. Having failed to excite as much interest as the Mustang generally, the final Falcon rolled off the production line in 1969 for the 1970 model year.

■ **ABOVE: The interior of a Falcon station wagon.**

Ford Model T

The Ford Model T, known affectionately as the Tin Lizzy, rolled off the production line and changed America's roads forever. The Model T put the country on wheels, helped build up the economy, and transformed a nation. With its blacksmith body panels (consisting of black Japan enamel) and crude instruments, the massed produced vehicle was the brainchild of engineer William C. Klann. Ford unveiled their Model T on October 1, 1908, and it set itself to become the most significant automobile the world had ever seen. It was designed as a touring car, but other body styles soon joined the first Model T, which wasn't produced for its beauty or speed.

The 177 ci (2.9 L) four-cylinder engine produced 20 hp and a top speed of 40 mph on America's dusty, unmade roads, while the gas tank sat underneath the front seat. The fuel was propelled through

the engine by gravity, and primitive cooling was provided in the form of a thermo-siphon. The Model T had a two-speed transmission operated by foot pedals and began with a modest production of 10,000 vehicles. By 1913, the Ford Motor Company was the largest manufacturer of automobiles – and produced around two million Model Ts from its factory each year by 1923. The original price of $825 was gradually reduced as more cars rolled off the production line, and by the time the company was building two million vehicles each year, it was possible to become the

proud owner of an automobile for as little as $260.

The real genius lay in the car's engineering, which was incredibly simple yet stunningly effective. The Model T had to be cranked in order to start the engine, although from 1919 an electric starter was optional. Once the engine was running, the spark was advanced before the driver could turn the ignition key. There was no foot accelerator and the driver had to release the hand brake before opening the hand throttle. A pedal was depressed on the left, urging the car into a low gear. The pedal was then released, once the vehicle was moving, in order to allow the transmission to shift itself into the higher gear. One fairly daring innovation of this cheap, tough model was the use of a removable cylinder head.

Ford Mustang

Since its launch in 1964, the Mustang has been, and still is, an iconic line and an integral part of US automobile history. Manufactured by Ford, it was based on the second generation of the compact Falcon. Now in its fifth generation, the Mustang was dubbed the 1964½ when it was unveiled in its first year in April at the New York World Fair. The company's highly successful model came in 1965 and both early Mustangs are cited as having introduced an American audience to the "pony cars." These vehicles were sports car-like coupes with short rear decks and long hoods and encouraged many generations of rival models from other automobile companies across the country.

The Mustang was designed by John Najjar as a prototype in 1961, known as Ford Mustang I.

a hatchback and coupe. The third generation was based on the Fox Platform, but sales fell in response to the 1980s spiraling fuel costs, and a fourth generation was introduced in 1993. It was the advent of a first major redesign in 15 years, based on the rear-wheel-drive Fox Platform, and a hatchback coupe model was reintroduced. From 2005, the fifth generation restyling harked back to the models of the late 1960s, powered by a 210 hp cast iron block 244 ci (4.0 L) SHOC V6 engine. Modifications and redesigns continued throughout the latter part of the first decade of the 21st century, and in 2012, the Mustang Boss 302 was introduced. This was followed by the Shelby GT500 later that same year.

43

Together with Philip T. Clark, the car was developed by Najjar and was formally debuted in October 1962 by Formula 1 racing driver Dan Gurney. Najjar is largely credited with giving the Mustang its name, although there are other citations with regard to where the name originated.

The models were modified and grew steadily larger and heavier for 10 years, before they returned to their original size in 1974 – the start of the second generation. For four years, the Mustang was available in a luxury Ghia version as well as

■ **ABOVE: An advertisement for the Ford Mustang, 1969.**

■ **LEFT: A Ford Mustang, 1972, with a more modern Mustang convertible.**

Ford Thunderbird

The Ford Thunderbird has been considered a classic icon of US automobile history since it made its debut in 1955. Produced as a rival to the Chevrolet Corvette, it appeared as a two-seater with a 292 ci (4.8 L) 212 hp V8 engine. The following year, horsepower was increased to 215-340 with a 312 ci (5.1 L) V8 engine, although the original was still available. By the 1958 model year, a four-seater was introduced to much critical acclaim. A further restyle came in 1961 and the Thunderbird was given a pointed front nose and modest fins, although the traditional round taillights were kept. A "Swing Away" steering column was another new feature.

The Jet Bird model line was brought in for the 1964 model year and the wheelbase was lengthened. However, the rooflines were shorter and the Thunderbird had a new design to the rear. A convertible was still available at this time, but the sports convertible was discontinued. Cosmetic changes came in 1965, with a reversed scoop behind the front wheels and a new front end. This was also the same year that power front disc brakes were

■ ABOVE: An advertisement showing the Ford Thunderbird, 1967.

■ OPPOSITE: A Ford Thunderbird, 1957.

■ BELOW: A Ford Thunderbird, 2002.

introduced. A new grille followed in 1966, and a single taillight – running the length of the back of the Thunderbird – complemented a new body. The standard 390 ci (6.4 L) engine was offered alongside a 428 ci (7.0 L), which was optional.

More dramatic changes came in 1967, with a new chassis and a four-door option. The headlight layout was changed (and concealed until switched on) and accompanied by a new grille. The convertible was discontinued in this model year. Another body change came in 1970 to the front bumper and grille, but it was 1972 before a new generation was launched. The luxury motor emphasized style and comfort and minimal changes came over the following few years. In 1976, however, Ford launched its largest and most luxurious Thunderbird to date, but this was reduced to a mid-range the following year. The 1977 edition involved a 302 ci (4.9 L) V8 engine as standard, although two larger engine options were available. The coupe was launched in 1983 – as a Thunderbird Turbo coupe – with a five-speed manual transmission and a turbocharged four-cylinder engine. That same year also saw the advent of a 305 ci (5.0 L) V8 engine, while aerodynamics were brought in by 1987, with the Thunderbird Sport and the Thunderbird LX. The Elan was quietly discontinued while the Turbo coupe remained the line's most popular model. Independent rear suspension was introduced with the 1989 Thunderbird, which offered a 232 ci (3.8 L) V6 engine. Models were dropped and changes came thick and fast during the following decade before production ceased in 1997. This popular model was briefly reintroduced in 2002, but when the last one left the factory in July 2005 there was no sign of a successor.

Lincoln Continental

■ OPPOSITE: The Lincoln Continental was known as the "Car of the Presidents." In this four picture combo we see the 1968 Lincoln Continental Presidential Limousine, top photo, the 1961, second from top, used by Presidents Kennedy and Johnson, the 1950 Lincoln, second from bottom, used by Presidents Truman and Eisenhower, and the 1939 Lincoln "Bubbletop," a specially built car used by President Roosevelt.

■ BELOW: The first Lincoln Continental, an offshoot of the Lincoln-Zephyr series developed under the leadership of Edsel Ford, 1939.

The Lincoln Continental enjoyed a long established history that began in 1939. Produced by the Lincoln Division of the Ford Motor Company, this highly-styled automobile was renowned for its luxury and decadence. The first Continental was intended as a personal, one-off model for Edsel Ford, or so the story goes. However, it is cited that if Ford liked the car it would go into production fairly quickly… which it did. The Continental was designed by Eugene T. Bob Gregorie in 1938 for Ford's personal use the following year. The template for the model was a Lincoln-Zephyr that was transformed into a convertible. Gregorie's design included a Lincoln V12 engine, a short trunk, long front fenders, and hydraulic drum brakes. It was long and low and it was sleek. The model was breathtaking in its appeal and, when Ford took his spring vacation, interest was high.

The first models off the production line were essentially the same and known as the Continental "Cabriolet" convertible. A very few hardtops were also added to the line. A limited number were produced in 1939, but are widely regarded as "1940 Continentals." Modifications over the first few years of production were minimal, but the length of the models was reduced in 1942. With new fenders and grille, the Continental became boxier and showed less grace, although maintained its position in the market despite America's direct involvement in the Second World War. However, after Pearl Harbor, production – for all American automobile companies – was suspended until 1945-46. Upgrades came post-war and the Lincolns from 1948 were the last to be produced with a V12 engine. As a result, the 1939-48 Continental is recognized as a full classic.

The Continental was relaunched in 1955 as a standalone line through the Continental Mark II. Luxury was a prerequisite, and this model was deemed exclusive. By the early part of the following decade, the Lincoln and Continental names were synonymous with this fourth generation marque and the car's size was undoubtedly a feature. The fifth generation came in 1970 and the sixth a decade later. However, the seventh generation came just two years later in 1982. Following the eighth generation, the ninth began in the mid-1990s when the Continental was given a substantial update. The Diamond Anniversary and the Spinnaker were both launched in 1996. The Limited Edition Continental came in 2001 and was followed by the celebratory Collector's Edition the following year. It was to mark the end of a long and successful history of the Lincoln Continental before the production line ceased operation.

Lincoln Mark Series

Ford was a leading manufacturer when they launched the luxury Lincoln Mark Series in the late 1950s. While the branding of all the Lincolns wasn't as straightforward and clear-cut as it is in the 21st century, the growth of this new line came about through development following the Lincoln Continental series. In 1956, Ford's Continental

in 1968. Thirty years later, the series came to an end as the final Mark VIII rolled off the production line.

Many of the series were produced as coupes and all were identified by a star logo, which originally came from the Lincoln Continental models. As far as Ford were concerned, all the Lincolns – which were not really identified as such – including the Mark series, came under the Lincoln-Mercury Division. The Mark II, a two-door hardtop coupe, was simple in its design but built to expected high standards by hand. The model came with power steering, power brakes, automatic transmission, and a high-spec interior, which included a motorized radio and power windows. It was marketed for $10,000 and was an expensive, if worthwhile, buy and came with optional air conditioning. Toward the end of the 1950s, the Mark III became a Lincoln, and sales improved on the Mark II model.

The Lincoln was now one of the largest vehicles on the road

and, by the time the Mark IV was introduced in 1959 and the Mark V in 1960, they were also some of the heaviest (with an extended wheelbase). The Mark IV and Mark V were not styled to the excess of the Mark III but, having been discontinued in 1960 as a series in its own right, the marque was reintroduced for the 1969 model year as – confusingly – the Lincoln Continental Mark III. The Mark IV (1972-76) was longer and wider than the Mark III, and powered by a 460 ci (7.5 L) engine. When the Mark V was launched in 1977, the 400 ci (6.6 L) became the standard engine – the 460 was optional (although later this was dropped when emissions testing deemed the engine unsuitable in California). However, the Continentals were only available with a 460 engine before the 400 became standard. Following the Mark VI (1980-83) and the Mark VII (1984-92), the Mark VIII was a rear-wheel-drive, which measured slightly larger than its predecessor. Its final models were made in 1998.

Division introduced the first Lincoln Mark series as a successor to the original Lincoln Continental. The series was produced between 1956 and 1960, but was later reintroduced

■ BELOW: A Lincoln Continental Mark II, 1956.

Nash/AMC Ambassador

In what was to become the company's flagship motor for AMC, the Nash Ambassador made its debut in 1927 as a sedan. It was based on model 267, the Nash Advanced Six, and went on to become one of AMC's senior lines between the early 1930s and late 1950s. It was part

LA SERIE NASH *Amba*

NUEVOS Y HERMOSOS MODELOS QUE EXPRE-SAN VERDADERO LUJO AUTOMOVILÍSTICO...A PRECIOS QUE SE PAGA-BAN ANTES POR COCHES MÁS PEQUEÑOS.

■ ABOVE: The Nash Ambassador.

of the company brand from 1958 until the mid-1970s.

The four-door high trim sedan had an expensive price tag at $2,090 and appealed to the rich and famous, including royalty, but was overtaken by other models from 1929 (which from 1934 included limousines). By the end of the 1920s, the Nash Ambassador was installed with a three-speed manual transmission and a 278.4 ci (4.6 L) OHV 16 engine. It was capable of 78 hp and was an integral part of the Advanced Six models until 1930. Two years later, Nash introduced the Ambassador Eight (which was to be a separate model range) and offered coupes alongside the sedan. This line came with straight-eight engines and was renowned for its high-class styling, quality, speed, and durability. In that same year, the company upgraded all models with new bodies and mechanics. Given the desperate effects of the Great Depression across the United States, surprisingly, the Ambassador sales remained in positive equity and Nash made a profit. New styling, known as the "Speedstream," was introduced in 1934, providing a touch of Art Deco, which was followed by more design changes in the form of "Aeroform" in 1935, and the addition of a two-door sedan in the Eight series. However, other changes included smaller, more compact models, and the first half of the 1930s brought about the end of the "big" classics.

Aerodynamics played a crucial role in design from the end of the 1940s, and post-war models were introduced with enclosed front wheels. Between 1949 and 1951, the Airflyte body was a popular Ambassador style, while 1950 saw the advent of the first AMC models to be fitted with Hydramatic automatic transmissions. The company was still edging, however, toward the compact car and a "small car" production line was implemented, leading to the Nash Rambler. The Ambassador underwent its last major restyling program in 1952, and the last model rolled off production in 1957. Despite this, the Nash Ambassador continued under AMC and Rambler brands until 1974. Many models – including the 1930 Series 490 and the 1932 Series 9-90 – are recognized as leading classics.

BELOW: A 1932 Nash 1082R Ambassador rumble seat coupe.

Oldsmobile 88 Series

■ ABOVE: An Oldsmobile 88, 1949.

■ OPPOSITE: The Oldsmobile 88, 1956.

First introduced in 1949, the Oldsmobile 88 – also known as the Eighty-Eight – was part of General Motors' Oldsmobile Division's remit for 50 years. It was a top-selling vehicle for nearly half its lifetime, between 1950 and 1974, and with its relatively light weight and V8 engine was a best performing car.

This full-size, or large car as it can also be termed, despite its fairly small body size, is considered a predecessor of the 1960s and 1970s muscle cars (particularly because of body size and large engine), although it has undergone many changes throughout its long-established history. Marques with the 88 badge, which was introduced in 1949, include the Futuramic, Super, Golden Rocket, Dynamic, Jetstar, Delta, Delmont, Starfire, Holiday, L/S, and Royale, amongst others. During the 1950s

and 1960s, it was common to refer to the models by their name and the number 88. The number replaced the 78 models and was introduced to work alongside the 76 and 98 models. With a powerful Rocket V8 engine, the Oldsmobile 88 was transformed from a fairly conservative vehicle into a competitive rival on the NASCAR circuits. It proved its worth with many wins throughout 1949 and the early 1950s and was dubbed the "King of NASCAR."

Following the end of hostilities of the Second World War, the Oldsmobile 88 became a firm favorite with ex-military personnel, who were used to operating powerful equipment. The first models were built with a starter push-button and an ignition key, which had to be inserted to unlock the ignition before the starter could be pushed. The two-piece

windshield was replaced by a single version in 1950, and the model won the Carrera Panamericana that same year. The 88 became the standard model in 1951, eclipsing the 76 models, and all were built with Rocket V8 engines, while the Super 88 made its debut that same year. Changes did follow in the next few years, but mechanically, apart from becoming more powerful, these were fairly minimal. A substantial facelift came in the mid-1950s, with new grilles, taillights, and chrome additions. The Rocket V8 was increased and a pillarless four-door was introduced. By the 1960s, there were name changes, while the 1970s saw the models restyled and enlarged. In the 1980s, changes were fairly minimal, while 1992 brought about the last redesign for the Oldsmobile 88 before it was discontinued seven years later.

Packard Super Eight

Hailing from Detroit, Michigan, the Packard Motor Car Company was responsible for the Packard Super Eight, a luxury model built between 1938 and 1951. The company had a long and illustrious history that began in 1899, and it was renowned for its luxury marques. Having developed the Packard models, by 1937 the company conceived the Packard 115C with a six-cylinder engine – a first for the company – and helped to bring the automobile manufacturer more in line with a mass market. Up to this point, Packard had been particularly exclusive and out of reach for a newly developed car-buying market. However, the introduction of the Six somewhat damaged the company's reputation as a luxury car builder.

By the Second World War, Packard were building airplane

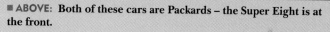

■ **ABOVE:** Both of these cars are Packards – the Super Eight is at the front.

■ **LEFT:** A Packard Super Eight, 1938.

engines, including the "Cadillac of the Skies," the P-51 Mustang Fighter. For GIs, it was one of the most powerful fighters of its time and was particularly reliable in combat. PT boats were also reliant on Packard, for their V12 marine engines, and the company

gained wide recognition for its war effort. However, back in domestic territory, the company was also developing the Packard Super Eight, the larger of two eight-cylinder luxury automobiles. There were some consistencies with the Packard Twelve, but from the 1940 model year onward the Super Eight was joined by a Super Eight One-Eighty, designed as a top-of-the-range vehicle. As a result, the Super Eight became the Packard Super Eight One-Sixty, with a 160 hp straight-eight engine.

In 1941, Packard developed a new top-class sedan with Clipper styling. The following year, this aspect was featured to include a Super Clipper and a Custom

Super Clipper, which both lasted in production for the next five years. Clipper was dropped from the marque's name in 1947, and the Super Eight One-Eighty became the Custom Eight and the Super Eight One-Sixty was renamed the Super Eight. Two years later, Packard launched the Super Eight Deluxe. In 1951, all models were renamed and the Super Eight became the 300. The straight-eight engine, with its smooth running reliability, was popular in luxury automobiles and racing cars alike, despite risks with "crankshaft whip," which could lead to the demise of the engine. Today, the straight-eight is unsuitable for modern vehicles due to the sheer length of the engine.

Plymouth Road Runner

Chrysler's Plymouth Division already had a GTX performance car when the concept of another muscle car was mooted. Designers went back to basics in order to conceive the Plymouth Road Runner, launched in 1968 for less than $3,000. The result was a low cost, high performance muscle car, which would far outstretch the GTX. Despite sometimes being confused with its forerunner, the Plymouth Road Runner was described as having "mechanical presence" over all other muscle cars on American roads. The Plymouth Road Runner Hemi was introduced in 1969 and made a dramatic impact on the streets, literally, with its loud exhaust and mesmerizing purr, which was more like a roar. Within months of the debut of the Road Runner, imitations were hot on its tail, but the Him Road Runner

■ LEFT & BELOW: A Plymouth Road Runner, 1969.

Performance was everything and mechanical improvements were carefully crafted to ensure the Plymouth Road Runner was the best in its class. Comfort and luxuries were overlooked to provide a cost-effective drive with powerful performance. Carpets were ignored in early models, basic vinyl and cloth seating was purely functional, and options were kept to a minimum. Between 1968 and 1970 the Road Runner was based on the Belvedere, with a 383 ci (6.3 L) V8 as standard. In the Hemi Road Runner, there was an option for a 426 ci (7.0 L) Hemi that would prove to be one of the best muscle car engines of all time. The four-speed manual came as standard, while the three-speed automatic was optional. Sales were more than double the company's expectations in 1968, when they reached 45,000. The Plymouth Road Runner – with its winning formula of high performance, low cost – was a competitor that even its sister company, Dodge, couldn't afford to ignore. In 1970, the Road Runner Superbird helped establish the NASCAR superspeedway for mainstream America.

held its own with its 335 hp 383 ci (6.3 L) four-barrel engine which came as standard. The top engine option was presented as a 425 hp 426 ci (7.0 L) Hemi Road Runner and accounted for 35 per cent of mid-size sales. Soon, a convertible model was launched, while power windows, front buckets, and a center console were offered as optional.

The car was named after the Road Runner character created by Warner Bros.; it cost Chrysler $50,000 to use the name and likeness of the popular cartoon.

Pontiac Firebird

The Pontiac Firebird took to the road in 1967 in the "pony car" range, styled on the Ford Mustang. It was a compact, reliable, and affordable vehicle with a sporty image that appealed to coupe buyers. The Firebird was favored for its high performance and even today is considered one of the most powerful cars ever available.

It has had an enduring popularity since the end of the 1960s, and its disappearance from the production line in 2002 was greeted with widespread dismay.

General Motors and its Pontiac Division had a large share of the market during the latter half of the 20th century. Engineer John DeLorean had intended that the

Pontiac Firebird should be a two-seater sports car, alongside the Chevrolet Corvette. However, GM had other ideas and, after several disappointing test-drives, the Firebird emerged, having been based on the four-seater Camaro. Despite this the Firebird had an identity of its own, with an engine set further back than the Camaro

■ **RIGHT:** The interior of a 1967 Pontiac Firebird.

■ **BELOW:** A Pontiac Firebird, 1967.

which enabled a better weight balance and rear traction bars. The Pontiac Division were renowned for their marketing and advertising and the Firebird was equally cleverly brought to public attention by the company with its five options.

A convertible and hardtop coupe were offered in the main model, which was quickly followed by the Sprint and the V8 Firebird 326, marketed as a "family sportster." The Firebird HO arrived with a four-barrel 326 ci (5.3 L), while the Firebird 400 could boast 325 hp. Each model was offered complete with options, and the starting price was only around $200 dearer than a six-cylinder Camaro. The first year of sales went well, despite a reduced debut season, and GM were pleased with results. In fact, the Firebird was so successful that it began looking as though it could take on the luxury pony car market – including the 1967 Mercury Cougar.

In 1968, a new 400 HO was introduced and elsewhere the mechanics were radically upgraded. The cars were powered by four-cylinder, six-cylinder, and V8 engines and, in 1969, the powerful Trans Am was launched. By this time, all the Firebirds had an extremely sporty look with lower-body styling that separated them from their Camaro template. The grille was now designed in a "bird beak" style and overall the car looked sleek and fast. However, restyling added significantly to the weight of the vehicles, although sales remained buoyant through the end of the 1960s with annual figures either on or close to 100,000 units. For a time, the Pontiac Firebird was dismissed as a glorified Camaro, but in the 21st century these classics have been reinstated as enthusiast "must-haves."

Pontiac GTO

For 10 years, General Motors built and manufactured the Pontiac GTO. The first model made its debut as a classic muscle car in 1964, designed by John DeLorean, Bill Collins, and Russell Gee. Pontiac prided itself on the model's street performance, brought about by a company ban

on automobile racing. Based on the Tempest, a new Super Tempest was designed with a 389 ci (6.4 L) V8 engine, with speed-mad youths in mind. The first GTO was an option package for the Pontiac Tempest and just 5,000 cars rolled off the production line to begin with. The

Ferrari 250 GTO was said to be the inspiration for the model's name, abbreviated from Gran Turismo Omologato, but was met with protests from enthusiasts. The 1964 model comprised a two-door coupe, in hardtop and convertible versions, and cost $4,500. The option package included a four-speed manual or a two-speed automatic transmission with additional tachometer if required.

■ BELOW & BOTTOM: A 1968
Pontiac GTO.

However, the major criticism that all the models received centered on the car's slow steering and many complained about the brakes, which were considered mediocre. Despite this, the GTO remained popular and there were many imitations on the market following its success. There weren't too many changes in 1966, but the following year saw various aspects in restyling, including four taillights to each side for the sports coupe, convertible, and hardtop. Sales continued to grow.

In 1968, General Motors redesigned the A-body, and the Endura front bumper was introduced, although customers could order the Endura Delete – which essentially meant the choice of a chrome front bumper and grille – while the standard engine became 350 hp at 5,000 rpm. Models underwent a facelift in 1970, and power steering was introduced – much to the delight of GTO enthusiasts. The following year there were further minor changes, but the Ram Air engines, which had been replaced earlier, were not returned as an option. Meanwhile, insurance premiums for muscle cars were on the increase and sales began to fall. By 1974, sales of all models were up slightly on the early part of the decade, but were significantly low enough to halt production of the GTO, (although a 21st-century line prevailed in Australia).

61

The "Bobcat" was born when Pontiac GTOs were modified further with a Bobcat kit and could achieve 0-60 mph in 4.6 seconds. The second year of production saw the GTO restyled with an additional 3.1 inches added to the length and the dashboard was changed. The 1965 model saw the three-speed manual as standard, while the four-speed manual and two-speed automatic remained optional.

Studebaker Commander

The Commander became a name synonymous with Studebaker between 1927 and 1966. Studebaker Corporation, known as the Studebaker Automobile Company, was an automobile and wagon manufacturer from Indiana. The company was founded in 1852 and had a long, illustrious history prior to the manufacture of the Studebaker Commander, first with electric vehicles before it established gasoline-powered engines. Renowned for its quality and reliability, the company began manufacturing gasoline automobiles in August 1912 and debuted the first Studebaker Commander in 1927, with a six-cylinder 226 ci (3.7 L) engine. The Light model, with its 40 hp 207 ci (3.4 L) straight-six, was based on a model manufactured by Studebaker known as the Special Six. It was joined by a Special model, with 50 hp 288 ci (4.7 L) engine, and the Big Six powered by a 60 hp 354 ci (5.8 L) straight-six. All three were considered tough, reliable, mid-range models.

This guaranteed worldwide recognition and the company introduced the President with an eight-cylinder engine the following year. (The first model named the President debuted in July some two years earlier in 1926.) The 1928 model was a smaller version with a 312.5 ci (5.1 L) engine, and quickly established itself as the premier car on the road. The Special, or Big Six, was succeeded by the GB Commander (in 1928), with a 354 ci (5.8 L) engine capable of 75 hp at 2,400 rpm. The Commander models went on to secure new Atlantic City Speedway records of up to 25,000 miles with a sedan (which averaged 62 mph) and two roadsters that averaged more than 65 mph. The showroom models had not been modified in any way, and proved their viability on America's hard roads.

The advent of improved roads across the United States saw the introduction of the Studebaker Dictator in 1937. It was followed by the Champion two years later, and by the end of the decade the Commander was marketed as a mid-range vehicle. The President model was dropped in the latter half of the 1940s and replaced by the coupe and the extended wheelbase Land Cruiser. In 1952, the State Convertible made its debut and the President was reintroduced three years later. While the Commander name was dropped in some years (namely 1936 and 1959-63), it made a comeback in 1964 on the Lark model. Studebaker ceased production of all its vehicles in the spring of 1966.

■ **ABOVE: The Studebaker Land Cruiser Commander, 1942.**

■ **OPPOSITE: Studebaker dropped the name Dictator in 1937 and replaced it with Commander to avoid any affiliation with Adolf Hitler.**

63

PLAYER'S CIGARETTES

STUDEBAKER
D' R DE LUXE SALOON

Clubs/Websites

AM Cruisers Car Club: clubs.hemmings.com/frameset.cfm?club=amcruisers

AMC Gremlin Club: cargurus.com/Cars/autoclub/home-amc-gremlin-ac1032

Cadillac Country Club: www.cadillaccountryclub.com/cadillac-deville.html

Checker Car Club of America: www.checkertaxistand.com

Chevy Classics: www.chevyclassicsclub.com

Chrysler 300 Club International: www.chrysler300club.com

Corvette Club of America: www.corvetteclubofamerica.org

DodgeCoronet.com: wwwdodgecoronet.com

Fairlane Club of America: www.fairlaneclubofamerica.com

Falcon Club of America: www.falconclub.com

Gateway Camaro Club: www.gatewaycamaro.com

Great Lakes Classic AMC Club: greatlakesamc.org

GTO Association of America: www.gtoaa.org

Hoosier AMC Club: www.hoosieramcclub.org

Impala SS Clubs of America: issca.org

International AMC Rambler Car Club: www.amcrc.com

International Thunderbird Club: www.intl-thunderbirdclub.com

Lincoln & Continental Owners Club: www.lcoc.org

Model T Ford Club International: www.modelt.org

Model T Ford Club of America: www.mtfca.com

Muscle Car Club: www.musclecarclub.com

Mustang Club of America: www.mustang.org

Nash Car Club of America: www.nashcarclub.org

National Firebird & Trans Am Club: www.firebirdtaclub.com

National Impala Association: www.nationalimpala.com

Oldsmobile Club of America: www.oldsmobileclub.org

Packard Club: www.packardclub.org

Packards International Motor Car Club: www.packardsinternational.com

Studebaker Drivers Club: www.studebakerdriversclub.com

The Camaro Club: www.thecamaroclub.net